Neural Networks for Complete Beginners

Introduction for Neural Network Programming

Mark Smart

Table of Contents

Disclaimer

While all attempts have been made to verify the information provided in this book, the author does assume any responsibility for errors, omissions, or contrary interpretations of the subject matter contained within. The information provided in this book is for educational and entertainment purposes only. The reader is responsible for his or her own actions and the author does not accept any responsibilities for any liabilities or damages, real or perceived, resulting from the use of this information.

The trademarks that are used are without any consent, and the publication of the trademark is without permission or backing by the trademark owner. All trademarks and brands within this book are for clarifying purposes only and are the owned by the owners themselves, not affiliated with this document. **

Introduction

Artificial neural networks are very common and popular in machine learning. This is because they help computers work like the brain of a human being. The concept of learning can easily be implemented with artificial neural networks. This book guides you on how to do this. Enjoy reading!

Chapter 1- What is a Neural Network?

A neural network is a kind of network in which the nodes are seen as "artificial neurons." The concept of the neural networks began in the 1980s. The neural network of the human being is made up of a network of interconnected neurons for maintaining a high level of coordination to receive and then transmit messages to the spinal cord and the brain. In machine learning, such types of networks are referred to as "Artificial Neural Networks (ANNs)."

The Artificial Neural Networks are made up of "neurons" which have been artificially created. These are then taught so that they can adapt to the cognitive skills of human beings. Some of the applications of ANNs are image recognition, soft sensors, voice recognition, time series predictions, and anomaly detection.

The Structure of Neuron

A neutron is made up of the cell body, having a number of extensions from it. The majority of these are in the form of branches commonly known as "dendrites."

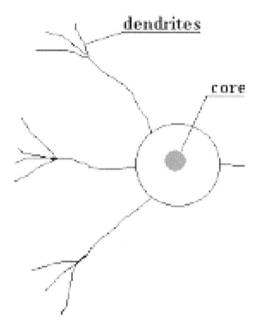

A long process or a branching exists, and this is referred to as the "axon." The transmission of signals begins at a region in this axon, and this region is known as the "hillock."

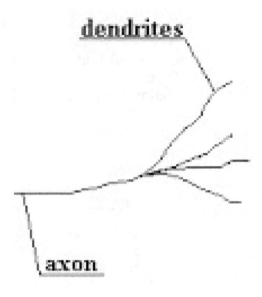

The neuron has a boundary which is known as the "cell membrane." A potential difference exists between the inside and the outside of the cell membrane. This is known as the "membrane potential."

If the input becomes large enough, some action potential will be generated. This action potential then travels and will then travel down the axon and away from the cell body.

A neuron is connected to another neuron by synapses. The information leaves the neuron via an axon, and is then passed to the synapses and to the neuron which is expected to receive it. Note that a neuron will only fire once the threshold exceeds a certain amount. The signals are very important, as they are received by the other neurons. The neurons use the signals or the spikes for communication. The spikes are also responsible for encoding the information which is being sent.

Neuron Input

Synapses can either be inhibitory or excitatory. When spikes arrive at the excitatory synapse, the receiving neuron will be caused to fire. If the signals are received at an inhibitory synapse, then the receiving neuron is inhibited from firing.

The synapses and the cell body usually calculate the difference between the incoming inhibitory and excitatory inputs. If this difference is found to be too large, the neuron will be made to fire.

Artificial Neural Networks

Suppose each neuron has a firing rate. Also, suppose each neuron has been connected to other m neurons and it is receiving m-many inputs in terms of x. From this, we can have a configuration which is known as a perception. It is a representation of some of the network models used in the early days. A perception usually models how a neuron works by taking a weighted sum for all the inputs and then sending the outputs, if the sum is found to be greater than the adjustable threshold value which is also known as the "activation function."

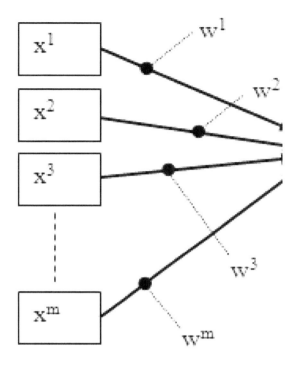

In our above case, the inputs are x1, x2, x3…xm, while the w1, w2, w3, and w4 are the real weights for these inputs, and the value for these can be either positive or negative. If an xi causes our perception to fire, this shows that the weight wi will have a positive value. If the wi inhibits the perception from firing, then its value will be a negative.

The perception is made up of weights, a summation processor, and the activation function.

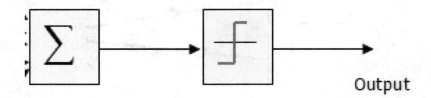

Output

In a perception, the bias can be seen as the propensity, or the tendency of behaving in a certain way, of your perception to fire regardless of the inputs.

The Activation Function

This function uses a number of functions. Let us discuss them:

Sigmoid Function

In this type of function, if the input is stronger, then the neuron will fire faster, or the firing rates will be very high. This type of network becomes very useful in the case of multi-layered networks since the sigmoid curve is capable of allowing for differentiation. Differentiation is highly needed in the case of a back propagation algorithm for the purpose of training the multi layer networks.

The Step Function

This function follows the following rule:

if 0 > x then 0, else if x >= 0 then 1

Chapter 2- Learning in Neural Networks

In artificial neural networks, learning refers to the process of modifying the bias and the weight. A perception works by computing the binary function for its input. The perception works by learning concepts. Learning in neural networks is facilitated by training it, whereby a certain set of inputs is fed to the network while expecting a particular output, which is the target output.

This calls for adjusting the values for the weights and the biases so that they can give us the target output. The training technique which is used in this case is referred to as the "perception learning rule." The process of learning in the artificial neural networks is similar to the concept of learning in human beings.

The Learning Rule

The training of the perception is done so that it can respond to the input vector with a target output, which can be either 0 or 1. For you to achieve a solution with the learning rule, a number of trials are needed, and there must be a solution.

Since learning is very central in artificial neural networks, it is good for one to choose the learning algorithm which is to be used. The activation rule in the neural network is fixed, and the same case applies to the target output since it's what we are targeting. Since these two cannot be changed, we have to change the values of the input weights. We therefore need a method which we can use to modify the weights in response to the changing inputs/outputs.

Note that once the input vectors are presented to the network and the answer is found to be correct, then no adjustment will be needed. If the output you get is not equal to your target output, then the weights should be adjusted. In this, an epoch refers to a complete pass of some input vectors.

You can present an input vector to the network at any time and you will be given a set of output vectors from this.

Supervised vs. Unsupervised Learning

In neutral networks, a learning algorithm can be either supervised or unsupervised. A supervised learning algorithm is the one in which the output has been given. During learning, an input pattern has to be provided to the input layer of the network.

This input will then be propagated through the network until we get an output. The target which is generated by the output layer of the network is usually compared to the target output. Based on the difference between the actual output and the target output, the value of the error is calculated.

The error obtained will show the learning effort of the network, and the imaginary supervisor is capable of controlling this. If the obtained error is too large, then the weights will have to be adjusted by a greater value, and the vice versa is true.

Learning in neural networks is said to occur if there are no target outputs. You can't determine or know what the targeted output will be like. In such a case, the inputs to the neural network are always arranged in a particular range, and this is determined by the input values which are provided. Your goal should be grouping of the similar units in some areas of the value range. This is a good measure for the classification of patterns.

We can also talk of reinforcement learning. In this case, the neural network relies on observation. It has to observe its environment, and it then makes a decision from there. In case the observation is found to be negative, the network will have to adjust its weight so that it can be in a position to make a different decision come next time.

The Back-Propagation Algorithm

For you to train a neural network so as to perform some task, the units of each unit must be adjusted so that we can reduce the error between the actual output and the target output. This means that the derivative of the weights must be computed by the network. To make it simple for understanding, the network has to monitor the changes in error as the weights are being increased or decreased. The back propagation algorithm is the one which is widely used in the calculation of this error.

If you have your network units being linear, then this algorithm will be easy for you to understand. For the algorithm to get the error derivative of the weights, it should first determine the rate at which the error is changing as the unit's activity level is being changed. In the case of the output units, the error derivative is obtained by determining the different between the real and the target output. To find the error change rate for the hidden unit in a hidden layer which is before the output layer, all weights between the hidden unit and the output units which it has been connected to have to be determined. We can then go ahead and multiply the weights by error derivatives in the weights and then the product is added together. The sum you get will be equal to the error change rate for the hidden unit. Once you have obtained the error change rate in the weights of the hidden layer which is just before the output layer, we will be capable of calculating the error change rate for the other layers.

The calculation of this for these will be done from layer to the next layer, and in a direction which is opposite to the direction in which the activities are usually transmitted through the network. This explains where the name "back propagation" comes from. After the error change rate has been calculated for some unit, the error derivative for the weights for all the incoming connections of the weight can be calculated more easily. The error derivative for the weights can be obtained by multiplying the rate of error change with the activity via the incoming connection.

Chapter 3- The Architecture of Neural Networks

Neural networks are classified based on their structure and how activities flow within. Let us look at some of the available neural networks based on their architectural structure:

Feed-forward Networks

These are a type of neural networks which allow the signals to move in one direction only, which is from the input to the output. In this type of network, there is no feedback or loops, meaning that the output from a particular layer does not affect it, that is, the same layer.

These are a kind of straightforward networks, simply because the inputs are directly associated with the outputs. They are widely used in purposes to do with pattern recognition. Such a type of an organization is known as top-down or bottom up.

Feedback Networks

These types of networks can have their signals flow in either direction, introducing the concept of loops in neural networks. These types of networks are very powerful, but this doesn't come for free, as they can be too complicated. They are too dynamic, in that their state keeps on changing continuously until an equilibrium point is reached. The network will then remain at that state of equilibrium until there is a new input, after which a new state of equilibrium will have to be found. Some people also refer to the feedback networks as recurrent or interactive networks.

The Network Layers

The most common type of an artificial neural network is made up of three groups which include the "input" units, which are connected to the layer named "hidden" units, and this layer is in turn connected to the "output" units.

The activity of the input inputs is a representation of the raw inputs which are fed to the network. The activity for the hidden unit is determined by the input units' activity and the weights which are connecting the input to the hidden units. The activity in the output units is determined by the activity in the hidden units as well as the weights which are connecting the hidden to the output units.

Note in this type of network, the hidden units are given a chance to represent their input units in their own way. The weights used between the input and the hidden units are responsible for determining the time that the hidden units will be active, and once these weights are changed, the hidden unit may choose what is to be represented.

In a single-layer organization, all the units are connected to one another. This forms the most common of organization in neural networks and it has a more computational power when compared to the hierarchy of the multi-layer organization. In the multi-layer networks, the units are numbered by the layers, and there is no global numbering which is used.

Chapter 4- Building Neural Networks

The artificial neural networks are inspired by the biological networks, and they are statistical learning models used in machine learning. The networks must be represented in the form of connected neurons which will send messages to each other. The network connections can be adjusted depending on the inputs and the outputs, and this makes the network ideal for supervised learning.

The neural networks can intimidate someone, and especially those with little or no knowledge of machine learning. For you to design a neural network, you should have an understanding of calculus and matrix operations. In this chapter, we will take you step by step on how to implement a neural network in JavaScript.

Training the Network

To train a neutral network means calibrating the weights by repeating two main steps. These are forward propagation and the backward propagation. Neural networks are very good in regression, and this explains why their best inputs are numbers unlike discrete values such as movie genres or colors, whose data is good for the classification of statistical models. The output data is usually in the form of a number in some range such as 0 and 1. However, this is determined by the activation function which is used.

During the forward propagation, a set of weights is applied to the input data and we then go ahead to calculate the output. Note that for the first propagation of the forward pass, the weights are selected randomly.

During the backward propagation, we have to measure the margin of the error of our output and then go ahead to adjust the weights based on the error that we get. The neural networks usually do both the forward and the backward passes, and the weights are calibrated accurately so as to predict the output.

Forward Propagation

In an XOR function, the mapping of the inputs to the outputs can be represented as shown below:

```
input    |      output

--------------------------

0, 0     |        0

0, 1     |        1

1, 0     |        1

1, 1     |        0
```

This function always gives the correct output, provided it was given input data which is acceptable by the XOR function. Suppose we need to use the last row in the above case, which is 1,1->0 so as to demonstrate how a forward propagation works.

We will use a single hidden layer, which is the layer between the input and output units. We should first have the following from this row:

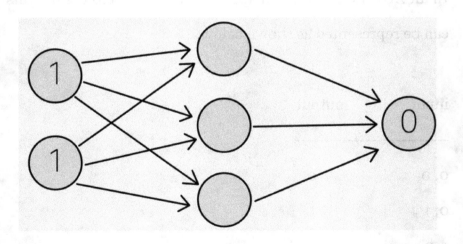

The input units are the ones labeled 1. The output unit is the one with a 0. The hidden units have not been marked. The weights in this case are the arrows. They have been used for connecting the units to each other. As we had said earlier, the first set of weights are chosen randomly, since it forms the first time we are doing the forward propagation. The values that you choose for the initial weights must be between 0 and 1, but your final weights do not have to be in this range.

Suppose we choose the values for the weights to be 0.8, 0.4, 0.3, 0.2, 0.9 and 0.5 from the first input at the top going downwards. We have to find the products of the weights and their corresponding inputs, and then sum them. This will give us the set of the inputs for the hidden layer. This is shown below:

$1 * 0.8 + 1 * 0.2 = 1$

$1 * 0.4 + 1 * 0.9 = 1.3$

$1 * 0.3 + 1 * 0.5 = 0.8$

Note that we have used three neurons in the hidden layer. There are two weights which lead to each of these hidden layer neurons. This is shown below:

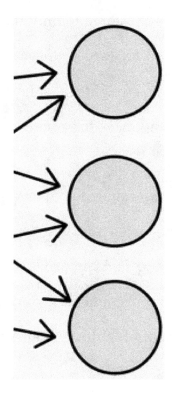

That is why we have to first get the product of each weight and the corresponding input. In this case, the input is 1, but the weights are different. That is why we are multiplying the value of the weight by 1 and then adding them. Note that only the weights which are leading to the same hidden layer neuron have been added.

For us to obtain the final values, we have to apply the activation function to the sums of the hidden layer. The activation function is responsible for transforming the input signals into the output signals, and this is necessary for the modeling of neural networks with non-linear patterns. There are several types of activation functions which include linear, sigmoid, hyperbolic, and others.

In this case, we will use the sigmoid function. This type of function takes the following formula:

$$f(x) = \frac{1}{1+e^{-x}}$$

Note that this function has to be applied to the sums of the hidden layer. This can be done as shown below:

S(1.0) = 0.73105857863

S(1.3) = 0.78583498304

S(0.8) = 0.68997448112

These can be represented as shown below:

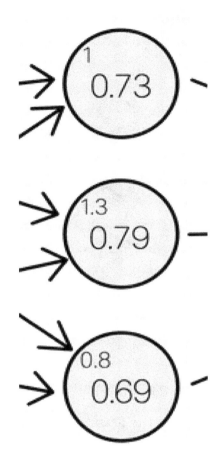

After doing the calculation, the weights connecting the hidden units to the output units will have the following values:

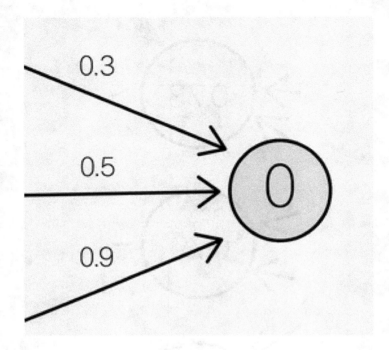

The sum for the result of the product of the weights from the hidden layer will give us the second set of the weights. These will help us to determine the sum of the output. This is shown below:

0.73 * 0.3 + 0.79 * 0.5 + 0.69 * 0.9 = 1.235

The above result should then be passed to the activation function so that we can get our final output. The activation function is a sigmoid and is shown below:

S(1.235) = 0.7746924929149283

This gives us the result given above. Our target output was 0, but the actual output is 0.77. Since we had chosen some random inputs, the output is off our target. If we stop at that point, then there would be errors in the weights of the neural network. This calls for us to perform a back propagation so as to find the error and adjust the weights!

Back Propagation

Before we can begin, we must determine the degree or the magnitude of the error from the target. After that, we should adjust the weights so that the errors can be minimized.

Similarly to what we did in the forward propagation, the calculations for the backward propagation have to be done at each layer. We have to begin by changing the set of weights which are between the hidden and the output layer.

The "output sum margin of error" is obtained by subtracting calculated output from the target output.

Output sum margin of error= target − output

Remember that our target was 0, but we got 0.77, so this can be calculated as follows:

0-0.77= -0.77

To determine the necessary change in the output sum, or the "delta output sum," we have to determine the derivative of the activation function, and we will then apply this to the output sum. In this example, our activation function is a sigmoid. This function will take the sum and then return the result.

S (sum) = result

The derivative of this sigmoid, which is called the sigmoid prime, will return the rate at which the activation function changes at the output sum.

S'(sum)= dsum/dresult

Since "output sum margin of error" refers to the difference in result, we can obtain the "delta output sum" by multiplying this with the rate of change.

$$\frac{dsum}{dresult} \times (\text{target result} - \text{calculated result}) = \triangle\text{sum}$$

This is an indication that the change in output sum will be similar to sigmoid prime for the output result. The mathematics for this can be done as follows:

Delta output sum = S'(sum) * (output sum margin of error)

Delta output sum = S'(1.235) * (-0.77)

Delta output sum = -0.13439890643886018

From the above calculation, the change proposed in the output layer is -0.13, and we can use this in the derivative of our output sum function so as to know the new change in the weights.

For remembrance, the "output sum" refers to the product between the result of the hidden layer and the weights which are located between the output and the hidden layer.

If there is a great change in output sum, there will be a great change in the weights, the input neurons which have a great contribution should have the biggest change in connecting synapse. The new values can be calculated as shown below:

hidden value 1 = 0.73105857863

hidden value 2 = 0.78583498304

hidden value 3 = 0.68997448112

Delta weights = delta output sum / hidden layer values (results)

Delta weights = -0.1344 / (0.73105, 0.78583, 0.69997)

Delta weights = (-0.1838, -0.1710, -0.1920)

old w7 = 0.3

old w8 = 0.5

old w9 = 0.9

new w7 = 0.1162

new w8 = 0.329

new w9 = 0.708

To get the change in our weights between input and the hidden layer, we will approach it in a similar manner. Also, it is good for you to be aware that only the initial set of weights will be used in the calculation as opposed to the ones which we have calculated above.

The following calculations will be necessary for us to determine the "delta hidden sum."

Delta hidden sum = delta output sum / hidden-outer weights * S'(hidden sum)

Delta hidden sum = -0.1344 / [0.3, 0.5, 0.9] * S'([1, 1.3, 0.8])

Delta hidden sum = [-0.448, -0.2688, -0.1493] * [0.1966, 0.1683, 0.2139]

Delta hidden sum = [-0.088, -0.0452, -0.0319]

Now that we have the value for the delta hidden sum, we can go ahead and then determine the change in the weights which are between the input and the hidden layer. This can be obtained once we divide this by input data (1,1). The input data in this case will be the same as the "hidden results" we obtained in the back propagation process so as to know the change in hidden-output weights. The calculations for this can be done as shown below:

input a = 1

input b = 1

Delta weights = delta hidden sum / input data

Delta weights = [-0.088, -0.0452, -0.0319] / [1, 1]

Delta weights = [-0.088, -0.0452, -0.0319, -0.088, -0.0452, -0.0319]

old w1 = 0.8

old w2 = 0.4

old w3 = 0.3

old w4 = 0.2

old w5 = 0.9

old w6 = 0.5

new w1 = 0.712

new w2 = 0.3548

new w3 = 0.2681

new w4 = 0.112

new w5 = 0.8548

new w6 = 0.4681

The new weights in comparison to the old weights will be as shown below:

old   new

----

w1: 0.8   w1: 0.712

w2: 0.4   w2: 0.3548

w3: 0.3   w3: 0.2681

w4: 0.2   w4: 0.112

w5: 0.9   w5: 0.8548

w6: 0.5   w6: 0.4681

w7: 0.3   w7: 0.1162

w8: 0.5   w8: 0.329

w9: 0.9   w9: 0.708

Now that we have the weights in their adjusted state, we can perform the next forward propagation. During the process of training a neural network, it is possible for one to make many passes, even thousands of them. If we use these values to perform a forward pass, the output will be 0.69, which is a bit closer to the targeted output. We will have done a single iteration on the neural network, but it will have helped us to improve the result.

We can then demonstrate how one can create a simple library in JavaScript showing how a neural network can be implemented.

The Mind

We can create a complete library to demonstrate how a neural networks works. This will involve more than just knowing how to perform a forward and a backward pass. We have to be aware of issues to do with APIs as well as how the use of the network will need to configure it. We want to demonstrate this by creating a simple neural network in JavaScript, and this will have a single hidden layer.

We should begin by creating a constructor function. This will be given the name "Mind." It is in this constructor that we will give the user the option of using either the hyperbolic tangent or the sigmoid activation function. The user will also be allowed to set the number of iterations they need, the learning rate, and the number of units that they need in the hidden layer. The constructor can be declared as shown below:

function Mind(opts) {

```
if (!(this instanceof Mind)) return new Mind(opts);

opts = opts || {};


opts.activator === 'sigmoid'

  ? (this.activate = sigmoid, this.activatePrime = sigmoidPrime)

  : (this.activate = htan, this.activatePrime = htanPrime);

// hyperparameters
this.learningRate = opts.learningRate || 0.7;

this.iterations = opts.iterations || 10000;

this.hiddenUnits = opts.hiddenUnits || 3;
}
```

In the above code, the "htan" represents the hyperbolic tangent sigmoid function. As you can see, we have used the keyword "opts" so as to give the user the option of using either the sigmoid or the hyperbolic tangent. Also, the user will have the choice of setting the number of iterations. The use of || is for commenting, so don't be bothered by these.

Forward Propagation

The forward propagation involves a series of sum products together with their transformations. We can now calculate the first hidden sum from the four input data. Again, our target is a o. Our inputs and their corresponding weights will be as shown below:

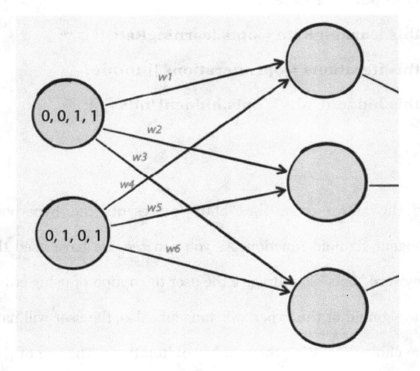

From this, to get the hidden layer sum, we will have to perform the following calculation:

$$
\begin{bmatrix} 0 & 0 \\ 0 & 1 \\ 1 & 0 \\ 1 & 1 \end{bmatrix} \times \begin{bmatrix} w_1 & w_2 & w_3 \\ w_4 & w_5 & w_6 \end{bmatrix}
$$

That is a matrix multiplication. That is why we said that you should have some knowledge about matrix multiplication. We will then have to apply a sigmoid function to the above sum so that we can get the result. This will give us the "hidden layer result."

We will then have to use the hidden layer result to get our final output result. This represents the entirety of the propagation code:

```javascript
Mind.prototype.forward = function(examples) {

  var activate = this.ac
tivate;

  var weights = this.weights;

  var res = {};


  res.hiddenSum = multiply(weights.inputHidden,
examples.input);

  res.hiddenResult                                =
res.hiddenSum.transform(activate);

  res.outputSum = multiply(weights.hiddenOutput,
res.hiddenResult);

  res.outputResult                                =
res.outputSum.transform(activate);


  return res;
};
```

That is the forward pass!

Back Propagation

This type of pass tends to be somehow complicated. We should look at our last layer and then determine the "output error." The following formula will be used:

Output sum margin of error = target – calculated

The following code will substitute for the above formula:

var errorOutputLayer = subtract(examples.output, results.outputResult);

We will then go ahead to configure hidden output changes. The code will be as follows:

var hiddenOutputChanges = scalar(multiply(deltaOutputLayer, results.hiddenResult.transpose()), learningRate);

Note that the changes are scaled by magnitude, learningRate, and this ranges between 0 and 1. The learning rate will apply a lesser or a greater portion of respective adjustment to your old weight. In case a large variability exists in the input, that is, only a little relationship exists between the training data, and the rate is set too high, the network may fail to learn well or it may not fail at all. If the rate is set too high, there is also the risk of "overfitting," or the process of training the network so that it can generate some relationship from the noise rather than the actual underlying function.

Because we are dealing with the matrices, the division can be handled by multiplication of the "delta output sum" with hidden results of the matrix transpose. This process will then have to be done again for the input to the hidden layer.

Note that in the backward pass, the result of the forward pass will be passed as the second argument. Here is the code for this:

```javascript
Mind.prototype.back = function(examples, results) {

  var activatePrime = this.activatePrime;

  var learningRate = this.learningRate;

  var weights = this.weights;


  // computing the weight adjustments

  var errorOutputLayer = subtract(examples.output,
results.outputResult);

  var deltaOutputLayer =
dot(results.outputSum.transform(activatePrime),
errorOutputLayer);

  var hiddenOutputChanges =
scalar(multiply(deltaOutputLayer,
results.hiddenResult.transpose()), learningRate);

  var deltaHiddenLayer =
dot(multiply(weights.hiddenOutput.transpose(),
deltaOutputLayer),
results.hiddenSum.transform(activatePrime));

  var inputHiddenChanges =
scalar(multiply(deltaHiddenLayer,
examples.input.transpose()), learningRate);


  // adjusting the weights
```

```
  weights.inputHidden = add(weights.inputHidden,
inputHiddenChanges);

  weights.hiddenOutput = add(weights.hiddenOutput,
hiddenOutputChanges);

  return errorOutputLayer;

};
```

The operations which have been used in the above code all come from a single npm module which was used before the matrix operations can be performed.

At this point, we have the codes for both the forward and the backward propagation. Our next step should be putting them together, and this can only be done by definition of a function which we will call "learn." This function accepts the training data in the form of an array of matrices. Random samples will then be assigned to the initial weights. A "for" loop will then be used for the purpose of performing the iterations and doing the forward and backward propagations. Here is the code for the "learn" function:

```
Mind.prototype.learn = function(examples) {

  examples = normalize(examples);


  this.weights = {

    inputHidden: Matrix({

      columns: this.hiddenUnits,

      rows: examples.input[0].length,

      values: sample

    }),

    hiddenOutput: Matrix({

      columns: examples.output[0].length,

      rows: this.hiddenUnits,

      values: sample

    })

  };


  for (var j = 0; j < this.iterations; j++) {

    var results = this.forward(examples);

    var errors = this.back(examples, results);
```

```
    }

    return this;

};
```

After that code, you will have learned how to create your own neural network and train it.

Chapter 5- The Perception

The perception forms the simplest form of neural network that we can have, and this is a computational model made up of a single neuron. It is made up of either one or more inputs, some processor, or then a single output.

It makes use of the feed-forward model, whereby the inputs have to be sent to the neuron, they are processed, and the output is given.

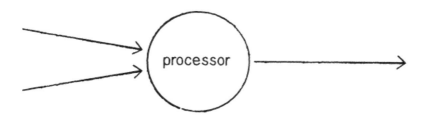

The following are the steps which are followed for processing in a perception:

1. Receive inputs

This is the first step in a perception. Suppose we have a perception which is receiving two inputs, x1 and x2. The values for these inputs are 12 and 4 respectively.

2. Weight the inputs

The inputs which have been sent to the perception have to be weighted. This involves multiplying the value of the input with a certain value ranging between -1 and 1. During the creation of a perception, one should first assign some random weights. Now that we have two weights, that is, weight 0 and weight 1, we will give them random values of 0.5 and -1 respectively.

We then have to multiply the inputs with their corresponding weights. This is shown below:

x1 * weight 0 = 12 * 0.5 = 6

x2* weight 1= 4 * -1 = -4

3. Sum the inputs

We can then get the sum of the weighted inputs. This is shown below:

Sum= 6 + -4 = 2

4. Generate the output

To get the output in a perception, we have to pass the above sum through an activation function. In the case of simple binary output, the activation function is responsible for telling the perception whether or not to fire. You can see this as a LED which has been connected to an output signal, if these fires, the light will go on, and if not, the light will stay off.

The Perception Algorithm

This involves the following:

1. For each input, multiply the input by its corresponding weights.

2. Get the sum of all the weighted inputs.

3. Compute the perception output depending on the sum which has been passed through the activation function.

Suppose we have two arrays made up of numbers, which are the inputs and the weights. Consider the example given below:

float[] inputs = {12 , 4};

float[] weights = {0.5,-1};

For each of the input, a loop will be needed so that in input can be multiplied by its corresponding weight. Since we need the loop, the results can be added up in that loop. Here is the loop:

```
float sum = 0;
for (int j = 0; j < inputs.length; j++) {
  sum += inputs[j]*weights[j];
}
```

Now that we will have obtained the sum, we can go ahead to compute for the output. This can be done as shown below:

```
float output = activate(sum);

int activate(float sum) {
  if (sum > 0) return 1;
  else return -1;
}
```

Note that the "activate()" function takes "sum" as the parameter, which means that we are passing the sum to our activation function.

Pattern Recognition with a Perception

Suppose you have a perception with two inputs, which are the x and the y coordinates of some point. By use of a sign activation function, the output for this will be either 1 or -1. The data for input will be classified based on the sign of output. The perception is as shown below:

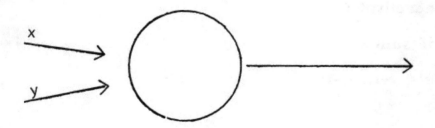

The two inputs to the perception are x and y, and the weights for these inputs will be weight x and weight y respectively. There is also a neuron to process this and generate the output.

What will happen if we add inputs of 0 for both x and y? The sum will always be 0 regardless of the weights that we choose. There is a need for us to protect against this problem. This can only be achieved by adding some 3rd input, which is normally known as the **bias.** The bias input usually has a value of 1, and it is weighted.

Once we add this input, we will have the following inputs:

0 * weight for x = 0

0 * weight for y = 0

1 * bias weight = bias weight

The output will be the sum of the three values given above and then plus the bias input. This will be 0 plus 0 plus 1.

Coding the Perception

We should now create the code for the "Perception" class. The perception needs data for tracking the input weights, and these can be stored in an array of floats. The class and the weights can be defined as follows:

class Perception {
float[] weights;

The use of [] shows that we are storing the weights in an array. The number of inputs can be passed as an argument to the constructor as well as the size of the array. The inputs in this case are x, y, and the bias. This is shown below:

Perception(int n) {
weights = new float[n];
for (int j = 0; j < weights.length; j++) {

```
    weights[j] = random(-1,1);

  }

}
```

The perception should be in a position to receive an input and then generate an output. We can create a function named "feedforward()" and then package these requirements into it. In our case, the perception will be receiving inputs in the form of an array, and the return value should be an integer. This is shown below:

```
int feedforward(float[] inputs) {
  float sum = 0;
  for (int j = 0; j < weights.length; j++) {
    sum += inputs[j]*weights[j];
  }
  return activate(sum);
}
```

The Perception object can be created and then made to guess for any given point. This is shown below:

Perception p = new Perception(3);

float[] point = {50,-12,1};

int result = p.feedforward(point);

The Perception object in this case has been named "p." Each weight has also been assigned some random value.

We cannot declare learning constant and give it the name "c," and then implement the training function for the perception as follows:

float c = 0.01;

void train(float[] inputs, int desired) {

 int guess = feedforward(inputs);

 float error = desired - guess;

```
for (int j = 0; j < weights.length; j++) {

  weights[j] += c * error * inputs[j];

  }

}
```

The variable c is responsible for control of the learning rate. The inputs have also been guessed, as well as a known answer. The error has been obtained by getting the difference between the desired output and the guessed value. The weights have also been adjusted based on the error and the learning constant.

The whole perception class will now be as follows:

```
class Perception {

  float[] weights;

  float c = 0.01;


  Perception(int n) {
```

```
  weights = new float[n];

  for (int j = 0; j < weights.length; j++) {

    weights[j] = random(-1,1);

  }

}


int feedforward(float[] inputs) {

  float sum = 0;

  for (int j = 0; j < weights.length; j++) {

    sum += inputs[j]*weights[j];

  }

  return activate(sum);

}


int activate(float sum) {

  if (sum > 0) return 1;

  else return -1;

}


void train(float[] inputs, int desired) {
```

```
    int guess = feedforward(inputs);

    float error = desired - guess;

    for (int j = 0; j < weights.length; j++) {

      weights[j] += c * error * inputs[j];

    }

  }

}
```

For us to do training on the perception, a set of inputs together with known answer are needed. This could be packaged in a class as shown below:

```
class Trainer {

  float[] inputs;
  int answer;

  Trainer(float x, float y, int a) {
    inputs = new float[3];
    inputs[0] = x;
```

```
  inputs[1] = y;

  inputs[2] = 1;

  answer = a;

 }

}
```

We can now pick some point and then determine whether it lies above or below the line. The formula for the line is shown below, where y is expressed as a function of x:

$$y = f(x)$$

Generally, a line can be written as follows:

$$y = ax + b$$

A processing function can then be written as follows:

```
float f(float x) {

 return 2*x+1;

}
```

Suppose we make up some point:

float x = random(width);

float y = random(height);

The function f(x) will give us the value of y in this line, and we can call it yline. This can be expressed as follows:

float yline = f(x);

The code for this is shown below:

```
if (y < yline) {
  answer = -1;
} else {
  answer = 1;
}
```

If the point y is above the line, the answer will be above the line. A Trainer object can then be made with the inputs and the correct answer. This is shown below:

Trainer t = new Trainer(x, y, answer);

The Trainer object has been named "t." Suppose we have a perception object named ptron, this can be trained by passing some inputs to it together with some known answer. This is shown below:

ptron.train(t.inputs,t.answer);

If we have an array of numerous training points, then the perception will work as follows:

Perception ptron;

Trainer[] training = new Trainer[2000];
int count = 0;

```
float f(float x) {

  return 2*x+1;

}


void setup() {

  size(640, 360);


  ptron = new Perception(3);


  for (int j = 0; j < training.length; j++) {

    float x = random(-width/2,width/2);

    float y = random(-height/2,height/2);

    int answer = 1;

    if (y < f(x)) answer = -1;

    training[j] = new Trainer(x, y, answer);

  }

}
```

```
void draw() {

 background(255);

 translate(width/2,height/2);


 ptron.train(training[count].inputs,
training[count].answer);

 count = (count + 1) % training.length;


 for (int j = 0; j < count; j++){

  stroke(0);

  int guess = ptron.feedforward(training[i].inputs);

  if (guess > 0) noFill();

  else        fill(0);

  ellipse(training[j].inputs[0],    training[j].inputs[1],
8, 8);

 }

}
```

Steering Perception

We want to make use of the concept of apperception so as to make an object with velocity, location, and acceleration. We will use the "ApplyForce()" function so as to move around the window. Here is the class:

class Vehicle {

  Perception brain;

  PVector location;

  PVector velocity;

  PVector acceleration;

We have created the attributes for the class, which include the location, velocity, and acceleration. A function for calculating the steering force is needed. We should then have the following:

```
void seek(ArrayList<PVector> targets) {

 for (PVector target : targets) {

   PVector force = seek(targets.get(j));

   applyForce(force);

 }

}
```

If you are located very far from the target, the force will be stronger. This is shown below:

```
void seek(ArrayList<PVector> targets) {

  for (PVector target : targets) {

    PVector force = seek(targets.get(j));

    float d = PVector.dist(target,location);

    float weight = map(d,0,width,0,5);

    force.mult(weight);

    applyForce(force);

  }

}
```

Suppose we need the brain to get all the inputs, process them based on the weights, and then come up with the output steering force. What if we have the following?

```
void seek(ArrayList<PVector> targets) {

    PVector[] forces = new PVector[targets.size()];

    for (int j = 0; j < forces.length; j++) {

        forces[j] = seek(targets.get(j));
    }



    PVector output = brain.process(forces);
    applyForce(output);
}
```

Suppose we ask the brain to take all the forces in the form of inputs, process them based on perception inputs, and then come up with the output steering force. This is shown below:

```
void seek(ArrayList<PVector> targets) {

  PVector[] forces = new PVector[targets.size()];

  for (int j = 0; j < forces.length; j++) {
    forces[j] = seek(targets.get(j));
  }

  PVector output = brain.process(forces);
  applyForce(output);
}
```

This means that instead of having to weight and accumulate the forces inside the vehicles, we just pass the array of forces to the brain of the vehicle object, and the brain will take the responsibility of weighting and summing the forces on our behalf. This output will then be used as a steering force.

If the vehicle needs to stay very close to the center, the brain will be trained as shown below:

PVector desired = new PVector(width/2,height/2);

PVector error = PVector.sub(desired, location);

brain.train(forces,error);

The copy of the inputs has been passed to the brain, and the observation regarding the environment. The inputs will need some correction to be done. The PVector is pointing from the current location to where there is a need for it to be.

The "error" vector can then help for adjustment of the values for the weights. The final code will then be as follows:

```
class Vehicle {

  Perception brain;
  PVector location;
  PVector velocity;
  PVector acceleration;
  float maxforce;
  float maxspeed;

  Vehicle(int n, float x, float y) {
   brain = new Perception(n,0.001);
   acceleration = new PVector(0,0);
   velocity = new PVector(0,0);
   location = new PVector(x,y);
   maxspeed = 4;
   maxforce = 0.1;
  }

  void update() {
```

```
  velocity.add(acceleration);

  velocity.limit(maxspeed);

  location.add(velocity);

  acceleration.mult(0);

}

void applyForce(PVector force) {

  acceleration.add(force);

}


void steer(ArrayList<PVector> targets) {

  PVector[] forces = new PVector[targets.size()];


  for (int j = 0; j < forces.length; j++) {

    forces[j] = seek(targets.get(j));

  }

  PVector result = brain.feedforward(forces);

  applyForce(result);


  PVector desired = new PVector(width/2,height/2);
```

```
    PVector  error  =  PVector.sub(desired,  location);
//[bold]
    brain.train(forces,error); //[bold]


}



    PVector seek(PVector target) {

    PVector desired = PVector.sub(target,location);

    desired.normalize();

    desired.mult(maxspeed);

    PVector steer = PVector.sub(desired,velocity);

    steer.limit(maxforce);

    return steer;

    }


}
```

Note that our vehicle has created a perception which will have n number of inputs and learning constant. All of our steering forces will be used as inputs, and that is why they have been passed to the "applyForce()" function.

Drawing Neural Network Diagrams

Suppose we need to draw the neural network diagram shown below:

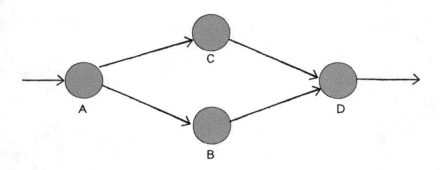

The above network is made up of neurons as the primary building units. We will then have a class named "Neuron" which will have x,y to describe the location of the entity:

class Neuron {

  PVector location;

  Neuron(float x, float y) {

```
    location = new PVector(x, y);

}


  void display() {
    stroke(o);
    fill(o);
    ellipse(location.x, location.y, 16, 16);
  }
}
```

The class is now capable of managing neurons in an ArrayList and has its own location. This is how the network and the neuron can be shown:

```
class Network {
  ArrayList<Neuron> neurons;
  PVector location;

  Network(float x, float y) {
    location = new PVector(x,y);
```

```
  neurons = new ArrayList<Neuron>();

}


void addNeuron(Neuron n) {
 neurons.add(n);
}


void display() {
 pushMatrix();
 translate(location.x, location.y);
 for (Neuron n : neurons) {
  n.display();
 }
 popMatrix();
}
}
```

The code for making our network diagram should be as shown
below:

```
Network network;

void setup() {
  size(640, 360);
  network = new Network(width/2,height/2);

  Neuron a = new Neuron(-200,0);
  Neuron b = new Neuron(0,100);
  Neuron c = new Neuron(0,-100);
  Neuron d = new Neuron(200,0);

  network.addNeuron(a);
  network.addNeuron(b);
  network.addNeuron(c);
  network.addNeuron(d);
}

void draw() {
  background(255);
  network.display();
```

}

The above code will display the nodes for us, but with no connections. We can use the "line()" function so as to add the connections. This can be done as shown below:

```
class Connection {

  Neuron a;
  Neuron b;
  float weight;

  Connection(Neuron from, Neuron to,float w) {
    weight = w;
    a = from;
    b = to;
  }

  void display() {
    stroke(0);
    strokeWeight(weight*4);
```

```
  line(a.location.x, a.location.y, b.location.x,
b.location.y);

 }

}
```

The function for connecting the neurons together should be written as follows:

```
void setup() {

  size(640, 360);

  network = new Network(width/2,height/2);


  Neuron a = new Neuron(-200,0);

  Neuron b = new Neuron(0,100);

  Neuron c = new Neuron(0,-100);

  Neuron d = new Neuron(200,0);


  network.connect(a,b);

  network.connect(a,c);

  network.connect(b,d);
```

```
network.connect(c,d);


network.addNeuron(a);

network.addNeuron(b);

network.addNeuron(c);

network.addNeuron(d);

}
```

You can then open the Network class and add a function named "connect()" which will connect together the neurons. This is shown below:

```
void connect(Neuron a, Neuron b) {

Connection c = new Connection(a, b, random(1));

}
```

For it to function, we must add an ArrayList of connections to the Neuron class. We should then go ahead to implement the addConnection() method for storing connections in the ArrayList. This is shown below:

```
class Neuron {

  PVector location;

  ArrayList<Connection> connections;

  Neuron(float x, float y) {
    location = new PVector(x, y);
    connections = new ArrayList<Connection>();
  }

  void addConnection(Connection c) {
    connections.add(c);
  }
```

We can then display our network diagram:

```
  void display() {
    stroke(0);
```

```
  strokeWeight(1);

  fill(0);

  ellipse(location.x, location.y, 16, 16);


  for (Connection c : connections) {

   c.display();

  }

 }

}
```

Conclusion

We have come to the end of this book. Neural networks embrace the concept of learning as in human beings. For a neural network to learn, training is needed. In this case, a set of weights is first provided to the network inputs. This first set is chose randomly, but the values should be between 0 and 1. Your aim is to pass these weights through the network and see the output they give so that you can compare it with the output you are targeting. The error computed determines the amount of adjustment which needs to be done to the weights so as to do away or minimize the error. This is called "training the neural network."

www.ingramcontent.com/pod-product-compliance
Lightning Source LLC
Chambersburg PA
CBHW061014050326
40689CB00012B/2639